3/16

AMICUS ILLUSTRATED • AMICUS INK

# DO YOU REALLY WANT TO MEET AN ELEPHANT?

WRITTEN BY CARI MEISTER    ILLUSTRATED BY DANIELE FABBRI

Amicus Illustrated and Amicus Ink
are imprints of Amicus
P.O. Box 1329
Mankato, MN 56002

Library of Congress Cataloging-in-Publication Data
Meister, Cari, author.
 Do you really want to meet an elephant? / by Cari
Meister ; illustrated by Daniele Fabbri.
   pages cm. — (Do you really want to meet?)
 Summary: "A child learns about domesticated el-
ephants and then goes on a trip to Sri Lanka to view
Asian elephants in the wild"—Provided by publisher.
 Audience: K to grade 3.
 ISBN 978-1-60753-733-5 (library binding)
 ISBN 978-1-60753-837-0 (ebook)
 ISBN 978-1-68152-007-0 (paperback)
1. Asiatic elephant—Juvenile literature. 2. Sri
Lanka—Juvenile literature. I. Fabbri, Daniele, 1978-
illustrator. II. Title.
QL737.P98M425 2016
599.67—dc23                        2014036129

Editor          Rebecca Glaser
Designer        Kathleen Petelinsek

Printed in the United States of America at Corporate
Graphics in North Mankato, Minnesota.

HC 10 9 8 7 6 5 4 3 2 1
PB 10 9 8 7 6 5 4 3 2 1

## ABOUT THE AUTHOR

Cari Meister is the author of more than 120 books for children, including the *Tiny* (Penguin Books for Young Readers) series and *Snow White and the Seven Dogs* (Scholastic, 2014). She lives in Evergreen, Colorado, with her husband John, four sons, one horse, and one dog. You can visit Cari online at *www.carimeister.com*.

## ABOUT THE ILLUSTRATOR

Daniele Fabbri was born in Ravenna, Italy, in 1978. He graduated from Istituto Europeo di Design in Milan, Italy, and started his career as a cartoon animator, storyboarder, and background designer for animated series. He has worked as a freelance illustrator since 2003, collaborating with international publishers and advertising agencies.

Here come the elephants. Aren't they grand?
Watch out! You wouldn't want to be stepped on.

Elephants are the largest land animals on Earth. The biggest elephants can weigh 15,000 pounds (6,800 kg)!

People and elephants have been partners for hundreds of years. Elephants are very strong. People train them to pull heavy things.

What's that? You really want to see a *wild* elephant? Okay. You have a choice. The largest elephants live in Africa. They have huge ears, and both males and females have tusks.

Or you could go to Asia. Asian elephants are
smaller than African elephants. Only male Asian
elephants have tusks.

You've always wanted to go to Asia?

Pack your suitcase! You're off to Sri
Lanka, the island nation south of India.
Both wild and tame elephants live there.

Wild elephants in Sri Lanka live in forests. Look for signs of elephants—like big round footprints.

Elephants are very good at being quiet and hiding.
It may be harder than you think to find one.

Why do elephants hide?

In Sri Lanka—like in many parts of Asia and Africa—people have taken over elephant land. Elephants have less and less space. This is a big problem for the herds. They have fewer places to eat grass. And they are forced to adapt to humans and—look out—busy roads!

Follow that elephant! But be careful and keep your distance! A threatened elephant is dangerous—both to humans and to other animals.

Elephants can kick, trample, and crush. Their
long, strong trunks can toss a human in the air.

When tracking an elephant, you need to keep a few things in mind.

#1 Elephants are unpredictable. You are never sure exactly what they are going to do.

#2 Elephants flap their ears when they are angry. Sometimes they just flap their ears to cool down.

#3 Elephants trumpet before they attack.

AND #4 They often "mock charge" before they are really going to attack.

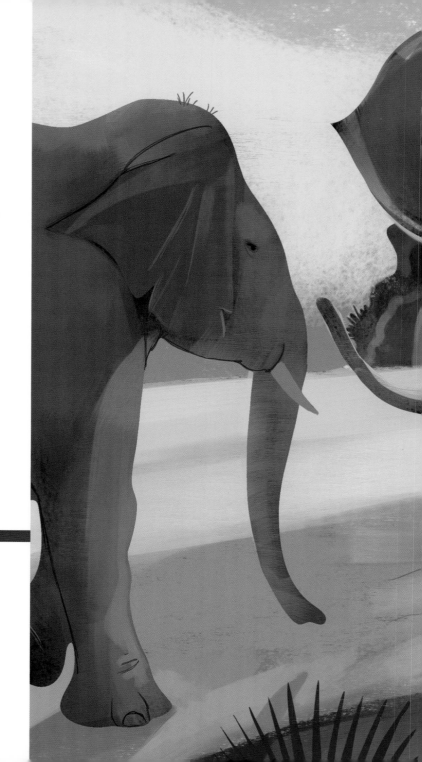

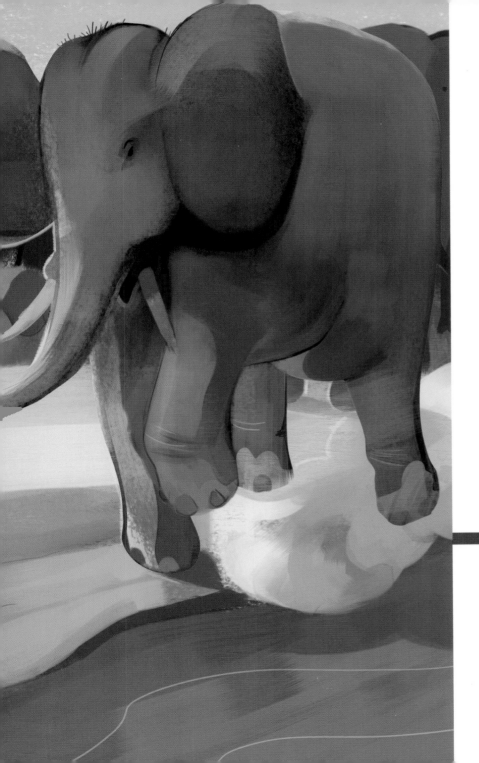

Hmm. It doesn't look like the herd wants to share the water spot. It's time to get out of here!

ELEPHANT ORPHANAGE

20

Now that you have seen some wild elephants, it's time to meet a tame one face-to-face. I think he likes you!

# WHERE DO ELEPHANTS LIVE?

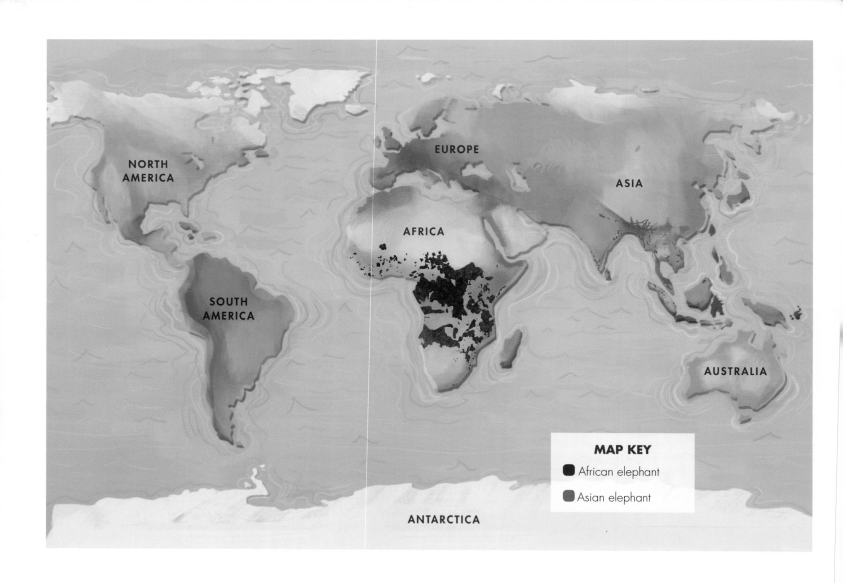

NORTH
AMERICA

EUROPE

ASIA

AFRICA

SOUTH
AMERICA

AUSTRALIA

**MAP KEY**
● African elephant
● Asian elephant

ANTARCTICA

# GLOSSARY

**adapt** To change to fit in or survive better in one's surroundings.

**herd** A group of animals that live together.

**mock charge** A pretend charge before a real charge or attack.

**trumpet** The sound an elephant makes.

**trunk** The long nose of an elephant.

**unpredictable** Not acting in a way that one first thinks.

## READ MORE

Downer, Ann. Elephant Talk: The Surprising Science of Elephant Communication. Minneapolis: Twenty-First Century Books, 2011.

Gagne, Tammy. Elephants. Minneapolis: Abdo Publishing, 2014.

Guillain, Charlotte. **Elephants**. Chicago, Ill.: Capstone Raintree, 2014.

Marsico, Katie. **Elephants Have Trunks**. Ann Arbor, Michigan: Cherry Lake Publishing, 2015.

## WEBSITES

Asian Elephant Videos, Photos, and Facts | ARKive
*http://www.arkive.org/asian-elephant/elephas-maximus/*
Watch videos of elephants in the wild.

Elephant Cam | San Diego Zoo Animals
*http://kids.sandiegozoo.org/animal-cams-videos/elephant*
Watch live elephant footage; learn about captive elephant behavior and more.

Just for Kids | International Elephant Foundation
*http://www.elephantconservation.org/stay-informed/just-for-kids/*
Print coloring pages, play educational games, and read up on fun facts about elephants.

National Geographic Kids: African Elephant
*http://kids.nationalgeographic.com/animals/african-elephant.html*
Listen to an elephant trumpet and see photos of elephants in the wild.

*Every effort has been made to ensure that these websites are appropriate for children. However, because of the nature of the Internet, it is impossible to guarantee that these sites will remain active indefinitely or that their contents will not be altered.*